The Grass Hisses

Dark Poetry for Troubled Minds

Nelson Mongiovi

All poems in this chapbook are copyrighted by the author

The Grass Hisses
Dark Poetry for Troubled Minds

© 2012 Nelson Mongiovi

Contents

Voices 3
Why So Dark 4
Mid Life Crisis 5
Old Wagon 6
Transition 7
My Haiku 8
First Therapy 9
It Just Happens 11
Anniversary 12
Family Photographs 13
Brick Mason 14
Blind Date 15
From a Distance 16
The Horizon 17
Observation 18
Knock Yourself Out 19
Troubled Son 20
Drug Intervention 21
The Expressive Drunk 22
The Anorexic 23
Baker Act: 24
Hope Diamond 29
Assisted Living 30
Mary Anne 31
After the Wake 33
At the Cemetery 34
Mirror 35
Wounding Words 36
Why the Words 37
The Hallway 38
Blue Crab 39
My Poetic Muse and Mentor 40
Objective 42

Voices

Some people
claim to hear voices.

I go a step further
and write what they say;

I create irrefutable evidence
that I am damaged.

Why So Dark

My poems are not meant to be written on frilly paper
gently folded and hidden in a jewelry box
to make you feel special.

I want to confiscate your artificial smile and
make you take that quick and confusing step backwards
as though you've stumbled across a dead body.

Each time you read a line I want the noose to tighten
and the words to crawl up your spine like spiders biting
with white-hot pain and burrowing under your skin.

Tear apart every sentence and let my madness spill out
so you will be contaminated and we can celebrate by
zipping up the body bag of what used to be you.

No, don't paste my work in your scrapbook;
cram it into the darkest corner of a drawer and
only pull it out when you need to feel normal.

Mid Life Crisis

Half a century old, I feel like
a starfish stranded on the shore
reaching for water
in five different directions.

A new shade of night
has descended upon me;
the weight of my choices
drips from my eyes.

Ruin has become a habit
impossible to break.
Only my shadow welcomes me
in the dim light.

My lucid moments
are no longer frequent
or as good
as the psychotic.

I hate this life
so deeply,
almost as deeply
as I love it.

Old Wagon

Peering over my shoulder
I light the fuse of remembrance

It sputters and
slowly moves ahead

To a tattered wagon
dragging behind me

Where I carry dreams
I never out-grew.

Transition

I have become rat-gray
in a maze of brilliant color.
My touch now leaves rust
on the shining effigies of youth.
Caught in a world where
opinions are wealth,
the air is thick
with bad ideas.

In nature
when an old mole is dying
the young
push him out of his tunnel.
Let's do this right
stand me up
spin me around
and ease the blade in.

My Haiku

The grass hisses

Yet I walk

Inviting the bite

First Therapy

Don't talk to me,
mouthing numb
psychobabble—
suggestions that I build
collages—scissor out
my torture from the *New
York Times* and *Hunting
and Fishing* magazines.

Don't talk to me
until you gag
as I have gagged
on my childhood's end—
where sin began.

Don't talk to me
until you are a thigh-
high boy, the perfect
size for his pleasure,
the back of your head
gripped by a greasy talon
that clutched and shoved—
your eyes wide open
to the bulge of his heaving
belly on your face.

Don't talk to me
until you taste his release—
the milky death of me—
the spewing salt
that brings me here—
an old turtle shell—a cold,
brittle cell cloaked
with veneer. I lived long
in this—crawled naked
toward your numb voice:

your poisoned honey voice,
seducing me with words of pretend
peace—another drone for your majestic
soft humming appointment book—
your lovely meter of money—
your perfectly rehearsed and deadly
sting of what you cannot know.

Don't talk to me!
Me, this potholed cavern
left behind in the grass
when I lumbered off to die;
unless you possess a proof
of my hell—until you produce
his corpse ravaged beneath
a transparent sheet—a tag
on his toe—and his sweet
juice of justice
on your own cheeks.

It Just Happens

I have awakened deaf
to the morning's chirping frost

Blind to bursting sunlight
without warning – feeling lost.

Anniversary

I awaken
wanting the dark taste of coffee
and the leftover poison
found in antique brown bottles
with skulls and crossbones –
Just a taste
of a hurt that never heals.

Reaching deep inside
I painfully remember
there are pieces that bite
and touching old memories
has the potential
to kill me –

Again.

Family Photographs

I do not live the fiction
or suffer the addiction
of families -- over-rated
where memories are jaded.

By pictures framed with lies,
convenient alibis, of
actions just before
the shutter closed its door.

I see motion – hear the sound,
as it wallows on the ground,
smell the black and rotting rose
and the pain behind each pose.

All conditioned to believing
there is merit in deceiving
and denying all the rages
never found in album pages.

Creating an illusion
without madness and confusion;
a reusable routine
concealing all -- that is obscene.

Brick Mason

I learned to lay bricks
at an early age
Taught that strong mortar
is always mixed
with practice and pain.

I shoveled and stacked
sealed brick upon brick
Built a fine fortress
blocking forever
possibility.

My side of the wall is
lonely and cold
I've run out of bricks
too tired, too old.

And so I begin
Chipping the hard lines
and prying out stone
Crawling through rubble;

Had only I known.

Blind Date

We sit together
in a mist of apprehension

Both pretending
we're not lonely

Silence
lays on the table before us

Like a dead cat.

From a Distance

An attitude in heels
she sits with him
on a park bench.

She touches his arm
and her eyes never drop
from mine.

The Horizon

I long to seize
the horizon.
Delusion
vivid and clear.

Darkness whitewashed
no shadows.

A tree line
amid no fear.

I leap at
the chance,
a wild cat.
Quarry pursued
in sight.

Possibility eludes
eager claws.
Futile
to capture
the light.

The chase
will resume
tomorrow.
Twitchy again
come near.

I long to seize
the horizon.
Waiting for it
to appear.

Observation

Death
silently stares
from the corner
of my room.

Inexplicably,
too many days
the only evidence
I am – alive.

Knock Yourself Out

Brush away pretense
kickstart desire;
Maybe you need to
get a little crazy.

Let down the locks
hike up your skirt;
The disguise
will keep you well hidden.

Go right ahead
be the life of the party;
I'll hold your hair
Later -
while you puke.

Troubled Son

A game from my youth,
we called it, "Trouble".
Two dice on a board,
sealed in a bubble.

Push on it hard,
they rattle and shake.
Wait for the numbers,
the path you must take.

We would play hard
and calculate odds,
knowing the outcome
was left to the gods.

You take the game further,
cast life in the dirt.
No place for the pieces
when taken or hurt.

No rules in your game,
or board for control.
It ends -- in an instant,
just one dreadful roll.

I feared you'd tossed snake-eyes
ten thousand times.
Each night my phone rang,
or the front doorbell chimed.

A uniformed stranger,
is speaking your name.
Stammering softly,
"He's ended the game."

I pick up your pieces
with horror and fright.
Trouble is over,
the box is closed tight.

Drug Intervention

See the white crow
waiting –
to be pecked to death
by others.

Those wise birds
puffed up and
perched above
like feathered trouble.

Their mental outing
is nothing more
than a murderous
nocturnal hunt.

Cawing insults
each talon --
poisoned
with bits of truth.

The fair one strains
for an absent branch
and falls further
into the dark forest.

The Expressive Drunk

Carefully picking
confusing memories
out of the trash,
I force myself to stay sober.

I once poured promises
into my glass
and tried to swallow,
the cruel bitter lies.

All that anger
drenching my soul
a deadly brew,
I now vomit on others.

Depressing words
with fancy flavors
loosely bottled and
labeled with gloom.

My dreadful drinking
was never a problem
until I was asked,

"Why did you quit?"

The Anorexic

I watched her eyes
butterfly across the lavish buffet
a body so gaunt
feeding on itself from within.

She settles
for nothing more than a drink --
equal parts of vanity and neurosis --
a tall glass of death.

Baker Act:
A Rhyme of Regret

Act I

Hundreds of eyes
drill the back of my head
I am shoved
behind a glass bubble.

Caged in the heat
on a cheap grimy seat
Missing door knobs
laugh at my trouble.

My job in descent
reputation - spent
In the time that it takes
to snap handcuffs.

Pushed up on a wall
patted down before all
No cunning to hide
from their rebuffs.

There's no flashing light
no siren… just fright.
If the windows could open
I'd scream.

The cop he won't talk
just the radio squawk
I'm convinced
this must be a dream.

Act II

Down a hallway of doom
to an unfurnished room
There's a cheap cordless phone
on the wall.

My head is now reeling
there's a lens near the ceiling
smirking, and
taping it all.

I grab for the phone
and dial up a drone,
"I'm sorry, we're not at home now."

The irony fits
I'm losing my wits
I must get away -
don't know how.

When, finally, a voice
(though not my first choice)
Spoke calmly and
seemed in command.

Said time and again,
"You know I'm a friend,
 You're all right, you're alright,
 It was planned."

Act III

Yes, I'd set the stage
in a pure drunken rage
It happened
the previous night.

A bottle in one hand
a gun from the nightstand
The end of my life
was in sight.

I'd put things in motion
now all the commotion
was clearly my fault
from the start.

A report had been filed
that I had gone wild
If not stopped, I would soon
fall apart.

Act IV

Now, I am on trial
they want blood in a vial
to see if I'm drugged
or insane.

Questions and forms
attack me in swarms
They're trying to
rattle my brain.

I give up my things
my goddamned shoestrings!
My belt and eyeglasses
as well.

A nurse takes my arm
patronizing, no charm
and escorts me to
my private Hell.

Act V

If you plug up your nose
and powder your clothes
You can get past the
smell of the room.

A mattress so thin
It's a damned loony bin
No pictures, or windows,
just gloom.

But, soon you meet others
your sisters and brothers
Where no one
acts like a pretender.

The stories they share
the feelings, the care
Will eventually
make you surrender.

It's safe in the "group"
It's where you recoup
and magical things
do occur.

When finally released
my addictions had ceased
My anger was
only a blur.

Act VI

On a follow up session
to check on regression
a Doctor allowed me
to read.

The files from my kin
who first put me in
And why they had
plotted the deed.

It read like a diary
with lines of inquiry
Of why I was such
a bad man.

They all expressed fears
I had hurt them for years
the evidence
held in my hand.

Finale

I'm feeling much older
and can't close that folder
I'm depressed and
in a black hole.

The liquor is top-shelf
I pour it for myself
And drink
to my bottom-shelf soul.

Hope Diamond

The stone smiles perfectly --
I am not moved.
Rather, the misery and misfortunes
it has visited upon possessors
arouses my soul.

The dark and depressing luster
is what I desire.
Unsteady shadows,
beauty
concealed in the curse.

I have always sought the story.
Within the blue,
there is blackness.
It is better
where I live.

The delicate gold filigree
clutches a strong and familiar pain.
A welcome flame
I kindle
for warmth and existence.

Labeled by many, a disease
dark diamond
brilliant, yet flawed.
I feel affection for torture;
a soul continually gnawed.

Assisted Living

The room has an airless quality --
hollow like
a lonely wooden boat
bumping against a dock
a misty-faced clock
marking time
and a television drones.

No one speaks
as crepe-paper hands
occasionally open
to bewildered faces
then fold again
in resignation.

They look tired
dozing away existence
in rhythm with the clock
tick-tock
        tick-tock
in that cold
and clammy room
where the sofa
smells of gloom --
and a television drones.

Like pigeons
in the winter
on a wire --
no one speaks.
They are huddled
against the chill
creeping on the floor
and kin that come no more
where the television drones.

It's a cold that never ends
brought by lovers,
colleagues, friends
to those that sit
from those that roam
all simply waiting
to go home.

Mary Anne

She knew
how to live.

Southern belle
sweet tea
formal silver.
Oddly possessed
with mean-spirited charm.

Her rust-clad golden years
were spent sleeping alone.
Touch deprived
with curls of wispy silver
craving the stroke of a gentle hand.

Four times a mother
twice a widow --
for the first time
she was frail.
Weakly complaining,
"I'm just so tired."

She knew
she was not going home.
Weary bones and spirit
silently weeping,
Recalling every moment
of her ten lifetimes – forever in pain.

Over the sickbay sensors,
voices called.
Home -- daughter -- dogs
All helplessly howling
for the injured
heart.

Finally,
etiquette elusive,
her body's basic needs
defaced, a portrait
of properness.

The glue for generations --
she no longer clings.
Dependence, a disease
she refused
to live with.

She knew --

      how to leave.

After the Wake

Tarnished treasure
strains the table
Weighted with dated
debris, from a stormy life.

Sour faces
politely plunder
amidst the rubble
that once defined – a woman.

Colorful sticky dots
Now bestow title
to a spirit within objects
they cannot carry home.

Death creates
peculiar boundaries
that reach beyond
the body's grave.

At the Cemetery

Grown cold
smothered in hate
A heart that
knew nothing of hope.

Among the plastic
faded flowers,
I smile
pretending to take note.

Finally lowered
from my sight
I am left listening
to the birds.

Mirror

Mirror in my face
righteous and anointed.
Reflecting my disgrace
proud and self-appointed.

Judge and sentence cruelly
without deliberation.
Uncaring and unduly,
with fierce determination.

Your surface only shows
my image cast from light.
Your backside must be dark,
two-faced and full of spite.

Through eyes wet with distress,
I see your goal much clearer.
And will not acquiesce,
to deception in the mirror.

Wounding Words

We speak with sharpened steel
painstakingly honed
and swift enough
to cut light.

All tender moments
scraped away by darkness.
Our self-taught survival
slips back to something feral.

Searing hot words
lead to icy cold sweats;
Terrified --
of what we will reveal.

__Why the Words__

The steady stream
of abusive filth
flowing from my mouth

The only thing

that stops my mind
from focusing on

the pain.

The Hallway

There is a hallway in my mind
where I smear my sins against you -- on a wall.
The doormat is soiled and smudged
from the countless times
I have been here before.
Atrocities flow like poisoned syrup
and slowly
ooze
down
 the
ugly
wall
settling on an unstable
and frightening floor.
The entire passage
is plastered with a black bitter frost.
Forgiveness is gasping
under the thick layers of pain
I have spread in this hellish room.
Please -- don't lock me in here -- forever.

Blue Crab

Enraged at being caught
stripped of all your fame,
Cornered and distraught,
this time you lost the game.

Greed became a prison
for angry painted claws;
You made a poor decision
your plan was full of flaws.

A victim and offended
now sensing your demise;
Your life has been upended
it's time to realize.

Desire is what trapped you
there's no one else to blame;
A cage is now your venue
this time you lost the game.

My Poetic Muse and Mentor

Unlike the wolf
that kills to exist
She is a cat
wanting nothing more
than to hunt for pleasure.

A polite scorpion
with stinging truths
that have inspired men
to art and madness.

She possesses
the poetic skills
to seduce a holy man
and instinctively knows
we are all hiding something;
most of the time, "something"
we want most.

A patient stalker
her smooth written words
can easily shock you
with just enough voltage
to hurt like hell
but not enough
to throw you from her lines.

My spunky little temptress
so well-proportioned
with flashing playful eyes
I enjoy the surrender.

Allowing her alluring voice
to seep from the nib of my pen
and expose her intentions
on a bed of fresh pages.

I will sit with her
listen to her
find in her
my demise.

Objective

I write
  secretly wishing
to paint
  darkness on the reader.

To prompt
  painful atrophy

A withering away
  of the mind and heart.

Stalking with words
  laced with Novocain

Wondering all the while,
  why am I numb?

Made in the USA
Charleston, SC
17 July 2012